chicken pickin'

by
Erik Halbig

PLAYBACK+
Speed • Pitch • Balance • Loop

To access audio visit:
www.halleonard.com/mylibrary

8135-4542-0363-6181

ISBN: 978-0-634-02528-0

HAL•LEONARD®

Visit Hal Leonard Online at
www.halleonard.com

Contact Us:
Hal Leonard
7777 West Bluemound Road
Milwaukee, WI 53213
Email: info@halleonard.com

In Europe contact:
Hal Leonard Europe Limited
Distribution Centre, Newmarket Road
Bury St Edmunds, Suffolk, IP33 3YB
Email: info@halleonardeurope.com

In Australia contact:
Hal Leonard Australia Pty. Ltd.
4 Lentara Court
Cheltenham, Victoria, 3192 Australia
Email: info@halleonard.com.au

Table of Contents

	Page	Audio Tracks

Preface

The term *chicken pickin'* describes a style of playing often used in (but not limited to) country music, and played mostly on a Telecaster-type guitar. This style was first popularized in the fifties and sixties by players such as James Burton, Jimmy Bryant, Roy Nichols (Merle Haggard), and Don Rich (Buck Owens). In the seventies and eighties, guitarists like Albert Lee, Ray Flacke, Ricky Skaggs, and Steve Wariner took it to another level. In the nineties, we heard exciting new ideas and playing by singer/guitarists Junior Brown and Vince Gill, but you can't talk about country chicken-pickin' in the nineties without the name of Brent Mason coming up. Mason has redefined the possibilities and raised the standards to which other players are compared. It will be exciting to see what this next decade will hold for the chicken-pickin' community.

This book touches on the basic techniques that define the chicken-pickin' style. Included are some scales that can help to inspire some new ideas. Bending is also very important in nailing the chicken-pickin' style. (Think about emulating the sound of a pedal steel guitar.) Open-string licks create a flowing, cascading sound that is used very often in this style of playing. Double-stop licks—licks that are predominantly played with two notes at a time—are also covered. The repetitive sequences are great warm-up exercises, but are also particularly effective in outlining chord changes.

The purpose of this book is to give you ideas on which you can expand. Take these ideas and change them to create your own licks. I hope this book inspires you to delve further into the exciting and ever-changing chicken-pickin' genre.

Chapter One

SCALES

MAJOR PENTATONIC

If there were one scale that defined country guitar, it would have to be the major pentatonic scale. It is the foundation from which country guitar is built and expanded. Here are the five basic patterns:

Fig. 1

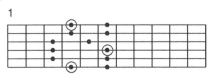

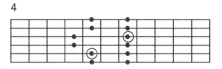

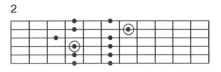

Here are some licks derived from these basic patterns:

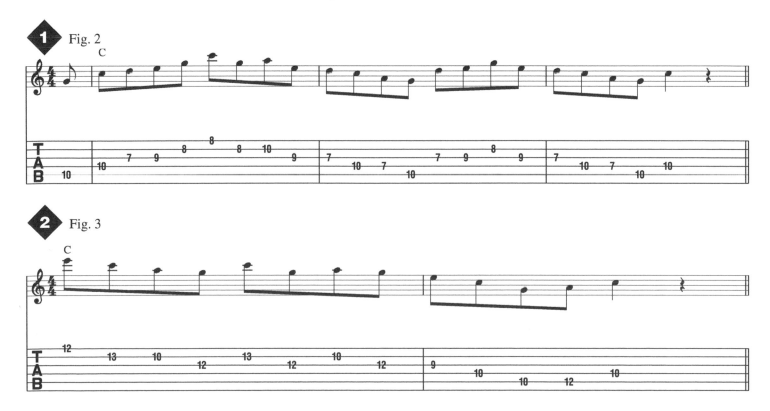

These patterns can be combined to extend the range of your lines. Play through these examples:

Fig. 4

1

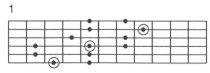

2

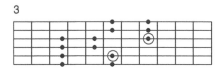

3

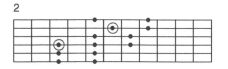

4

5

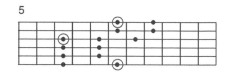

Here are some licks incorporating the combined patterns:

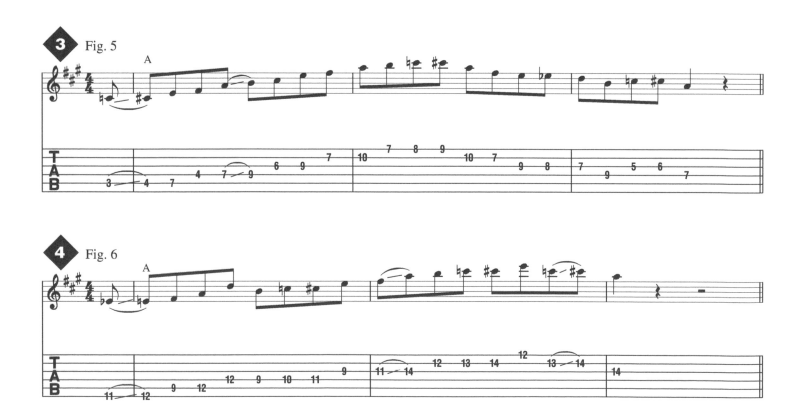

COUNTRY PENTATONIC

This next scale is derived from the major pentatonic scale. I changed one note to make it sound a little hipper. It now reads: 1, ♭3, 3, 5, 6. Here are the five basic patterns:

Fig. 7

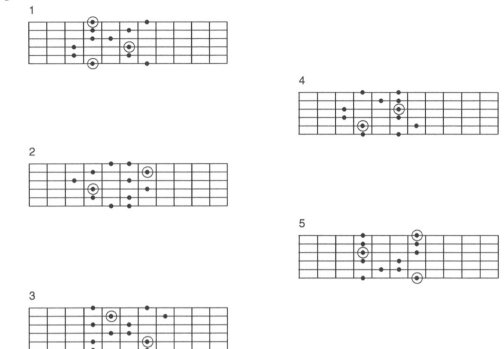

Try these licks derived from the country pentatonic scale:

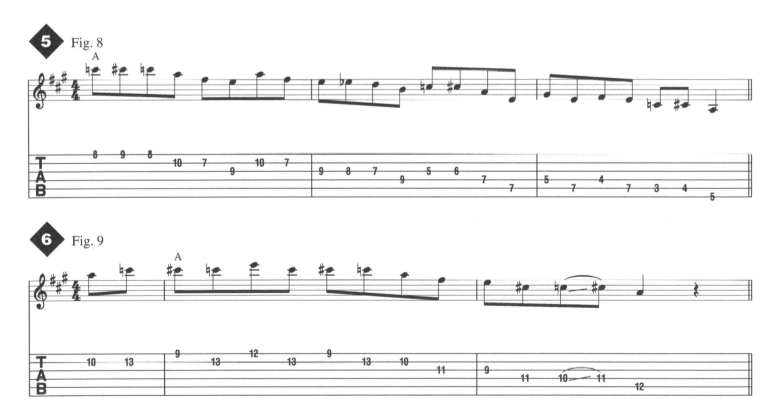

ROOTLESS DOMINANT PENTATONIC

For those of you with inquiring minds, here is an interesting scale that will jazz up your country lines a bit. Try this one on a western swing or even a quick train-beat type tune. It works great! The pitches are as follows: 3, 5, 6, ♭7, 9. Here are the five basic patterns:

Fig. 10

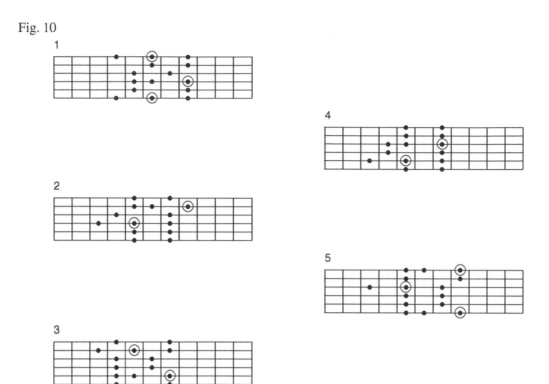

Check out these licks derived from the rootless dominant pentatonic:

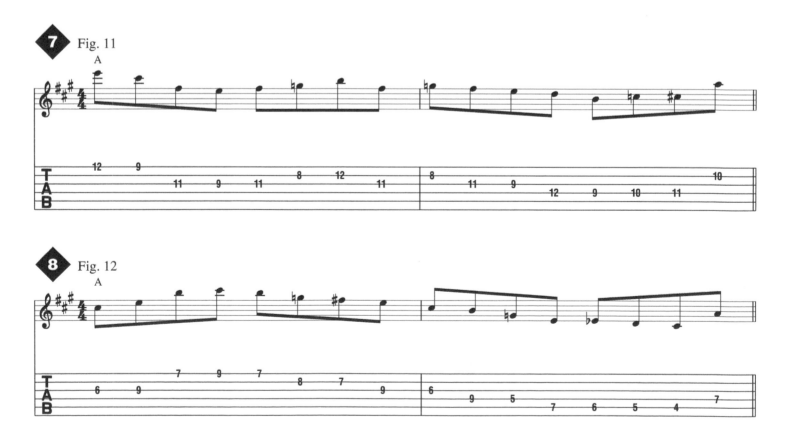

MIXOLYDIAN #2

Check out how you can alter one note and make the Mixolydian mode more useful as a country scale. The pitches are: 1, #2, 3, 4, 5, 6, ♭7. Here are the seven basic patterns:

Fig. 13

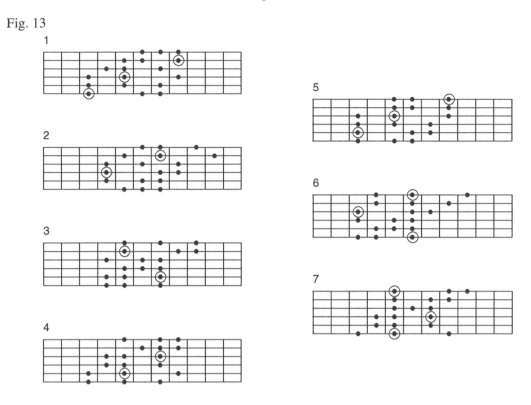

Try out some licks derived from the Mixolydian #2 scale:

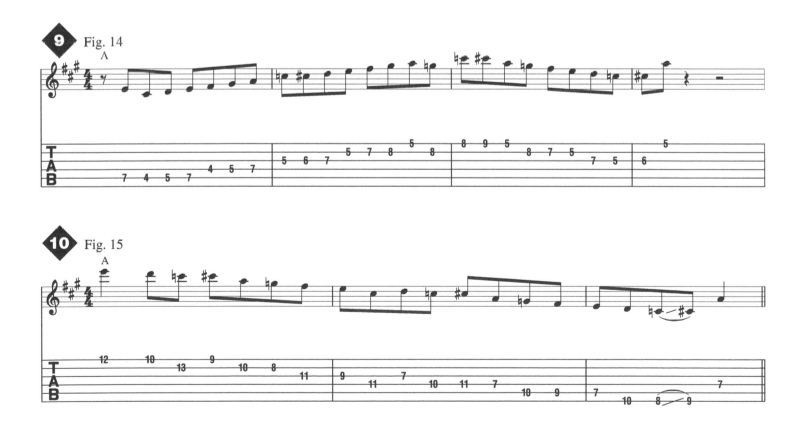

STRING SKIPPING

If you are looking for some exciting new sounds that will challenge you technically, this is the section for you. Play through these examples and see.

Fig. 16

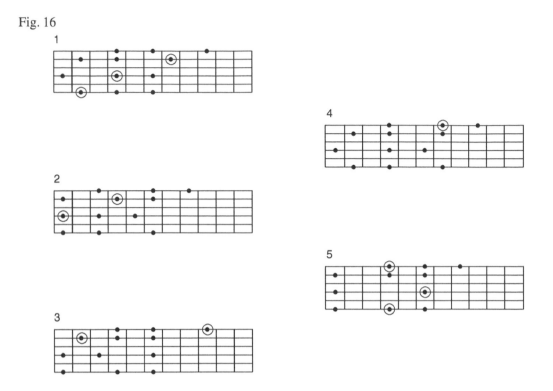

Here are some licks based on this concept:

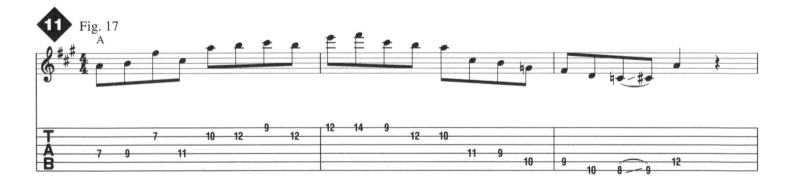

Chapter Two

BENDING

Bending is approached quite differently in country guitar playing than in blues or rock. The main difference is that in country, when you bend a note, you will more than likely hold that note up and play some notes on another string while you are holding it. Here are a few examples. Bend the second degree to the third. Then, on the adjacent higher string, grab the fifth, then the fourth.

13 Fig. 19

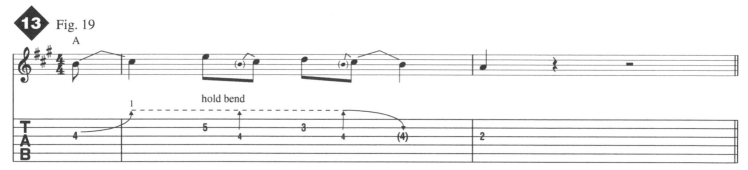

Try grabbing the fourth before the fifth, with the second bent up to the third:

14 Fig. 20

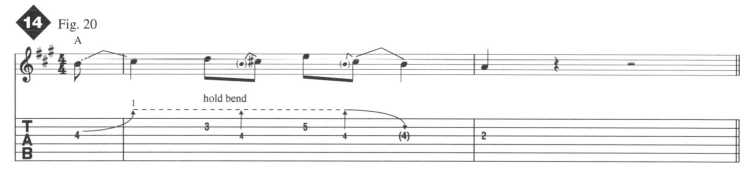

You can also bend the fourth to the fifth and grab the root, then add the flat seventh:

15 Fig. 21

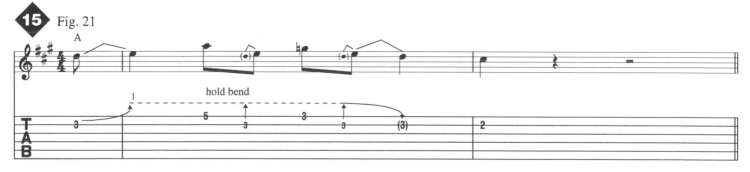

Or, you can grab the flat seventh and then the root, with the fourth still bent to the fifth:

16 Fig. 22

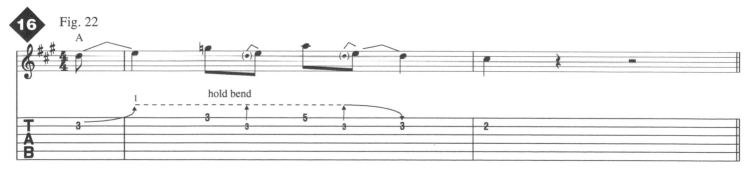

Bend the flat seventh up to the root; grab the third above, then the second:

17 Fig. 23

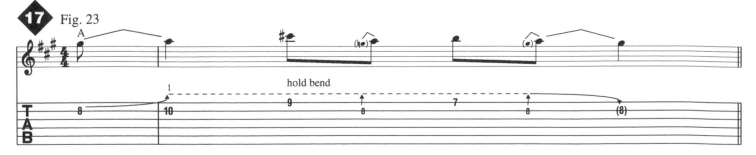

With the flat seventh bent up to the root, grab the second, then the third:

18 Fig. 24

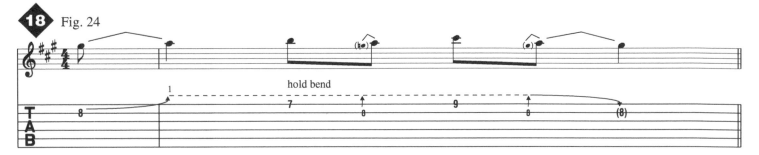

You don't always have to grab notes on adjacent strings when you have a note already bent. For example, try bending the second to the third on the third string. Then grab the root and then the flat seventh on the first string:

19 Fig. 25

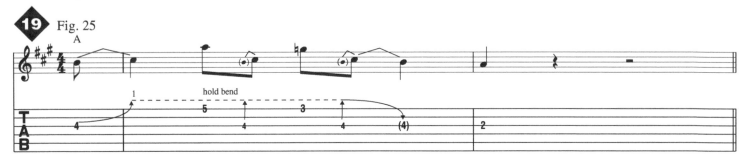

With the same note bent, substitute the sixth for the flat seventh:

20 Fig. 26

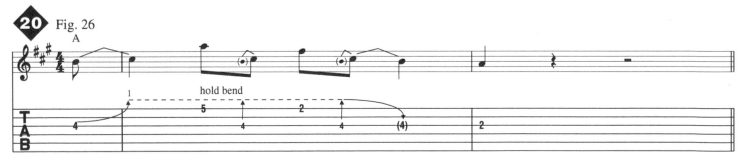

Again, with the same note bend, grab the flat seventh first, then the root:

21 Fig. 27

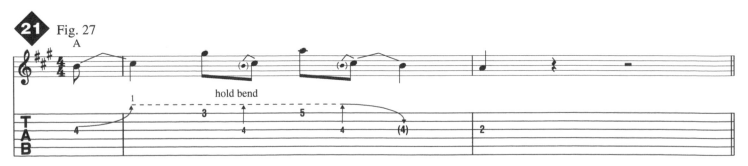

Here is another idea that you can use with the second bent to the third: try grabbing the sixth, then the fifth

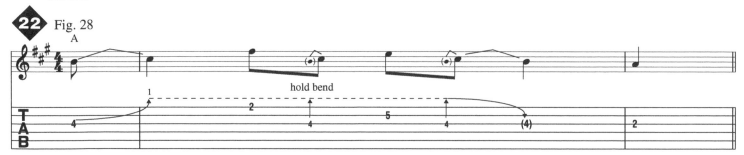

Or you can grab the fifth, then the sixth:

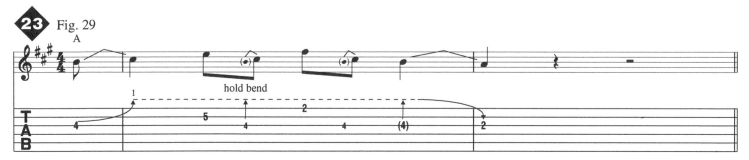

All of the bending licks covered here can be played with harmonics to sound even more like a pedal steel guitar. Another interesting idea you can try is to link some of these licks together and work your way horizontally up and down the neck. Here's a descending idea:

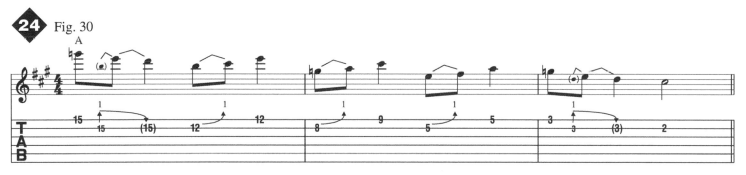

You can embellish this idea by adding extra notes:

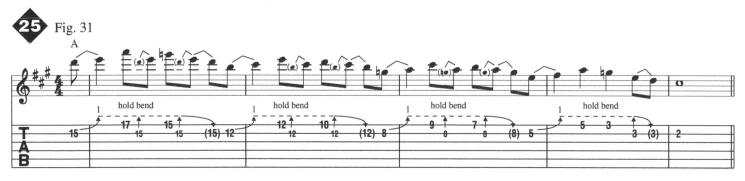

Try this idea using non-adjacent strings:

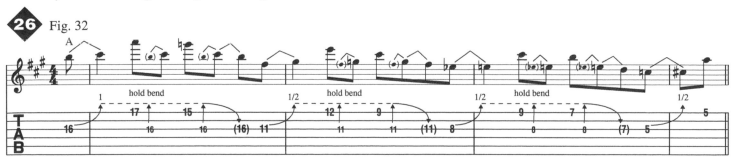

Unison bends are an effective way of getting from one end of the neck to the other:

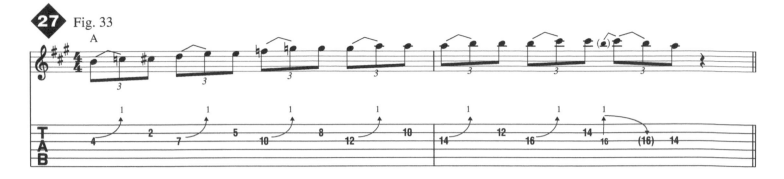

PLAYING THROUGH CHORD CHANGES

Try this next exercise to test your bending precision. We are going to outline three different chords:
E, A, and B. Over the E chord, bend the F♯ to G♯ (second to third) on the third string, then grab the E
to D (root to flat seventh) on the first string. To outline C♯ (fifth to third) on the first string. over the B
chord, bend F to F♯ (flat fifth to fifth) on the third string and grab the D♯ then C♯ (third to second) on the first
string.

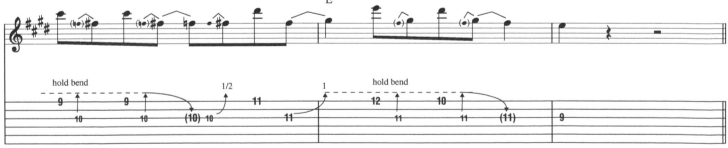

Chapter Three

OPEN-STRING LICKS

These licks are made up of open strings ringing out against fretted notes, creating a cascading effect. Here is how you would play a G major scale:

29 Fig. 35

Obviously, to play these types of runs, you need to play in keys that contain the notes of the open strings. The best keys are E, A, D, G, and C. Certain licks work better as ascending runs. I will give a few examples of each, in each of these keys. Here are a couple of descending licks in the key of E:

30 Fig. 36

30 Fig. 37

(cont'd)

You can expand on that idea too!

31 Fig. 38

Here are some ascending runs in E:

Fig. 39

Fig. 40
(cont. d)

These descending ideas sound good in the key of A.

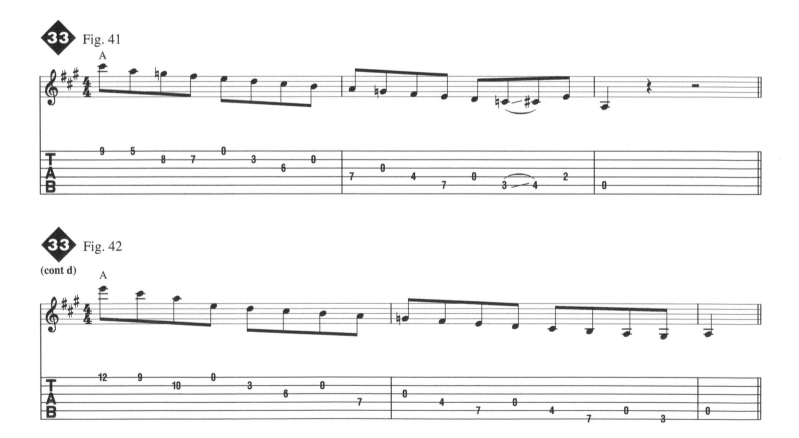

Fig. 41

Fig. 42
(cont d)

Try these ascending licks in A:

34 Fig. 43

In the key of D, you can play these descending ideas...

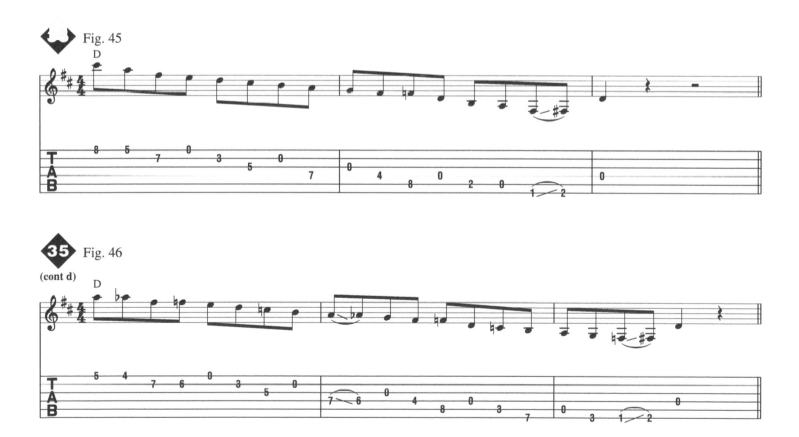

Fig. 45

35 Fig. 46

...or these ascending ones:

Here are some interesting descending licks in G...

...and some ascending licks in G:

Play through these descending licks in C...

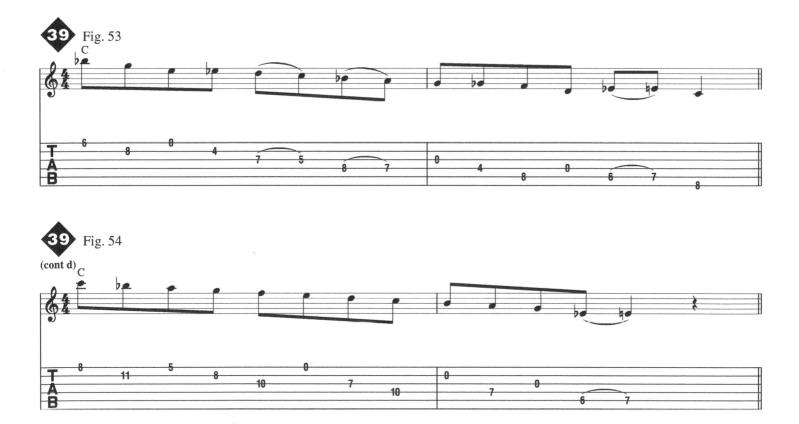

...and these ascending ones:

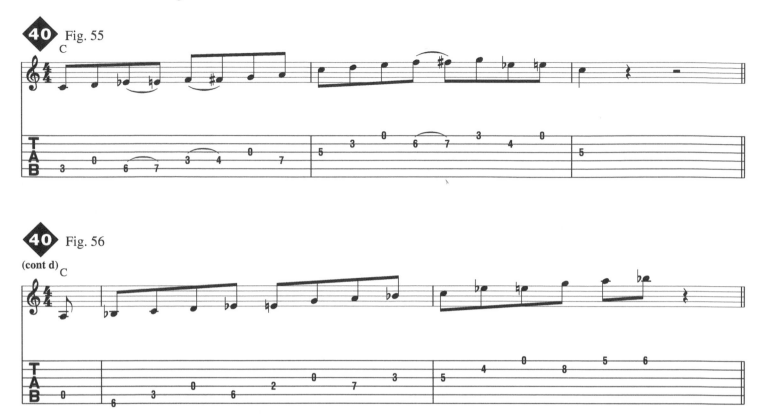

Believe it or not, you can get some pretty interesting cascading open-string licks in the key of B as well. Try this descending example:

Here is an ascending lick:

I came up with a few repetitive licks that outline chord changes. Try these examples in the key of E over the I and IV chords:

Here is an exercise that incorporates the ideas we've been discussing in this chapter, also in the key of E over the I and IV chords.

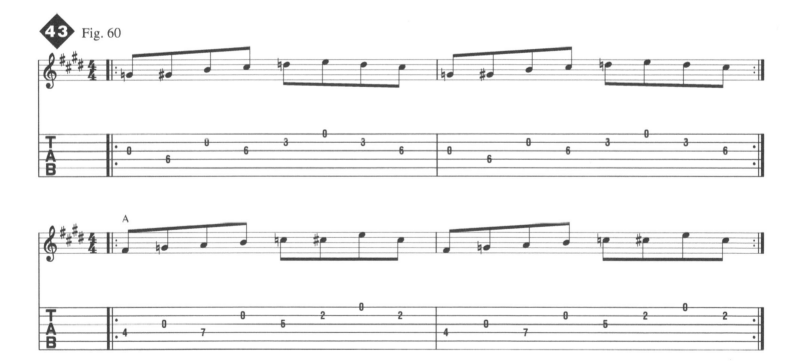

Chapter Four

DOUBLE-STOP LICKS

The term *double stop* refers to two notes being played (stopped) at the same time. The intervals most commonly used are thirds, fourths, fifths, and sixths. Let's begin by harmonizing the major scale in thirds:

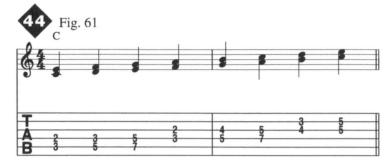

Now let's harmonize in fourths:

Now let's harmonize in fifths:

And last, we'll harmonize in sixths:

With these intervals, you can create some very interesting solos. As we all know, however, anything used in excess can become boring. So what I like to do is develop licks that incorporate various different intervals. The first two figures are ascending licks (in the key of D) made up of thirds and fourths:

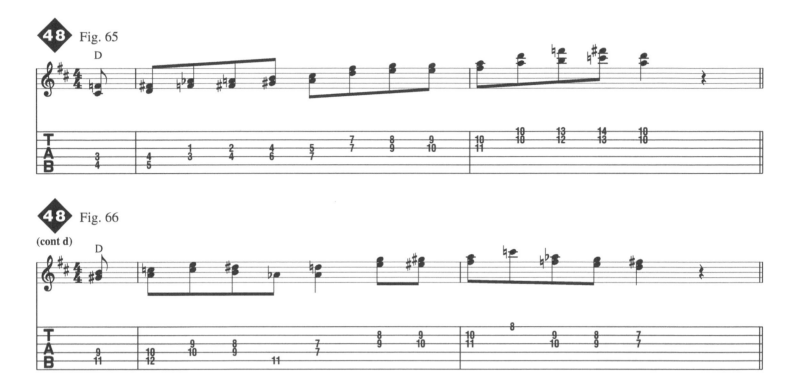

Next is a descending lick in A, made up of major- and minor-third intervals (and also one major-second interval):

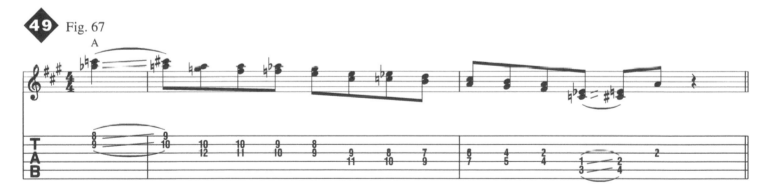

A lot of my licks incorporate one or more single notes along with double-stop notes. This first one is in the key of A:

Here's one in G:

Here are some licks that incorporate bends with double-stop licks:

Another cool technique you can try is the use of pedal points. For those of you who don't know, a *pedal point* is a note that is repeated while other notes move under, over, or around it. Here are some examples in various keys:

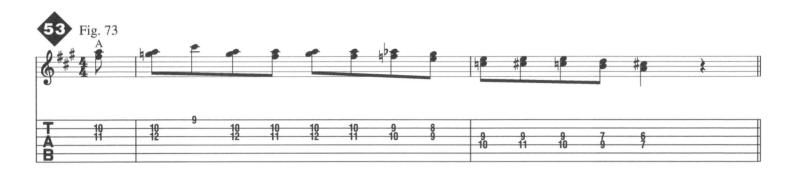

These licks are all in the key of A:

57 Fig. 77

58 Fig. 78

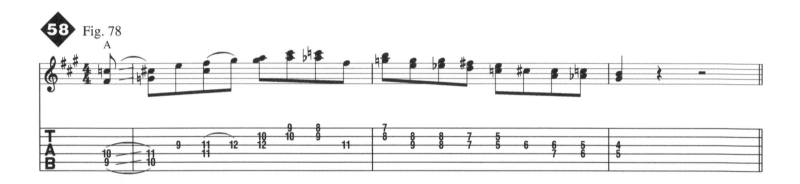

59 Fig. 79

60 Fig. 80

Chapter Five

REPETITIVE SEQUENCES

In this section, we will focus on short, one- or two-measure phrases that repeat and outline the chords over which you are playing. These ideas work especially well over quick train-groove tunes.

The first two examples outline the I and IV chords in the key of G:

Fig. 81

The next two examples are variations on the first two. There are many possibilities...

Fig. 82

If you want to take this a step further, here are a couple examples in which I've added the sixth to spice it up a bit. This lick covers the I and IV chords in the key of E:

Fig. 83

Here are some two-measure phrases. This example outlines the I and IV chords in the key of G:

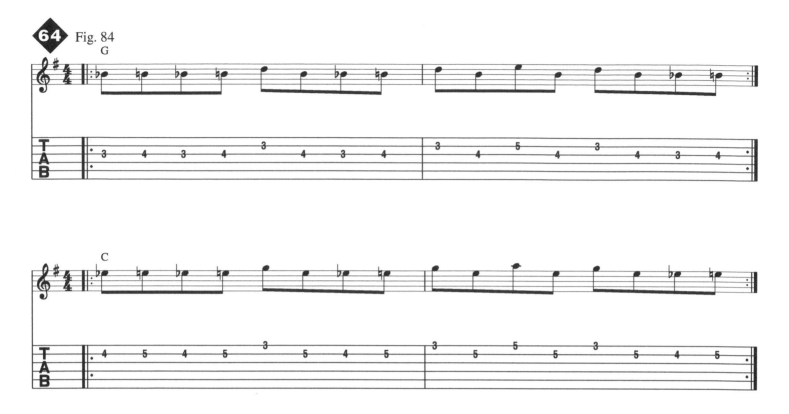

This one outlines the I and IV chords in E:

Here are some other one-measure variations in G. The first one covers the I and IV chords:

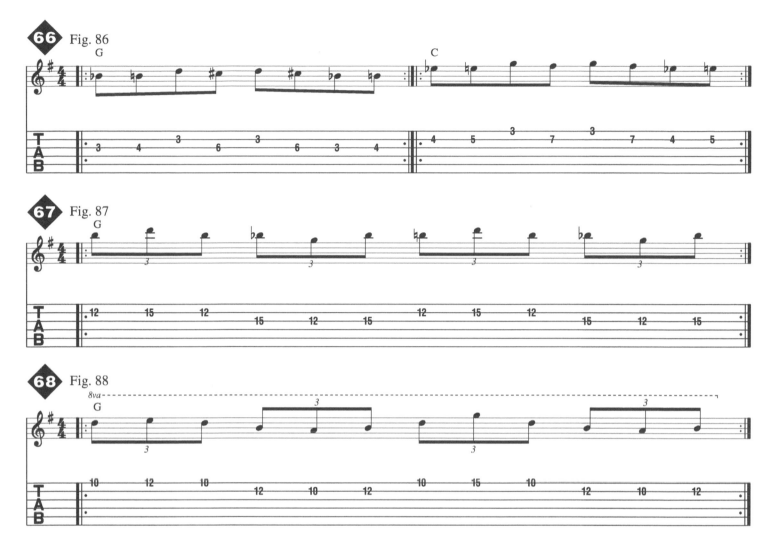

The next three licks outline the I, IV and V chords (respectively) in the key of E, and are very challenging to play at quick tempos:

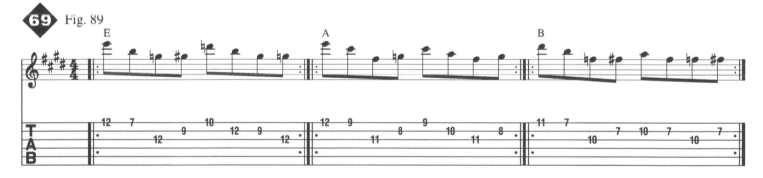

Here are a couple of two-measure phrases that outline the I and IV chords in the key of C:

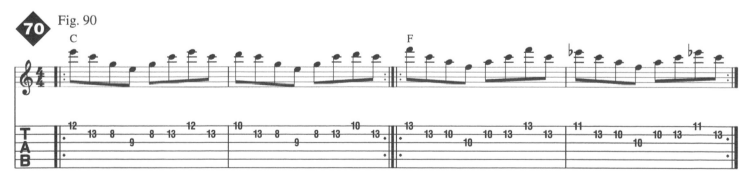

You can play some pretty interesting repeating figures on one string. These licks will require some stretching. Here are three ideas you can play over the I, IV and V chords in the key of E:

71 Fig. 91

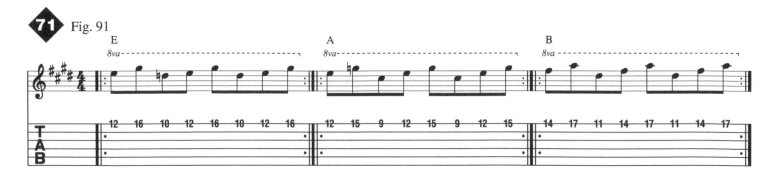

Here are some two-string repeating figures that outline the I, IV, and V chords in the key of A:

72 Fig. 92

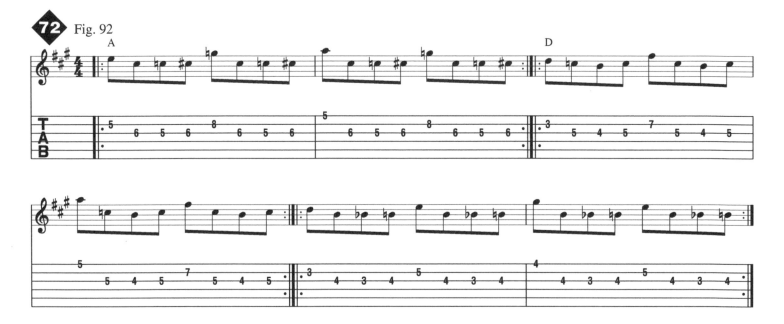

If you are feeling up to some big stretches and string skipping, check out these examples which again outline the I, IV, and V chords in the key of E:

73 Fig. 93

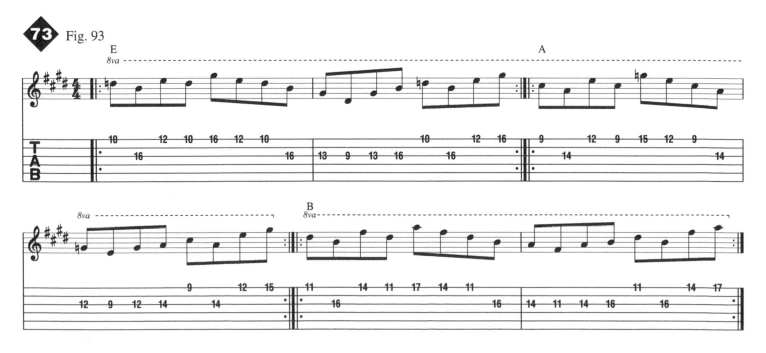

Here are some variations:

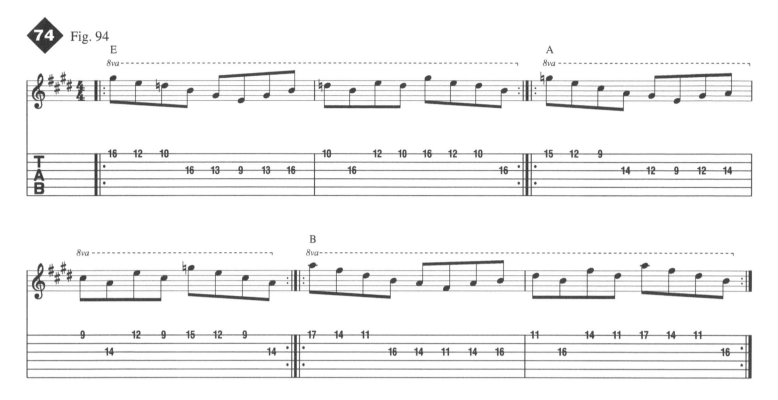

Try these repetitive double-stop licks over the I and IV chords in the key of E:

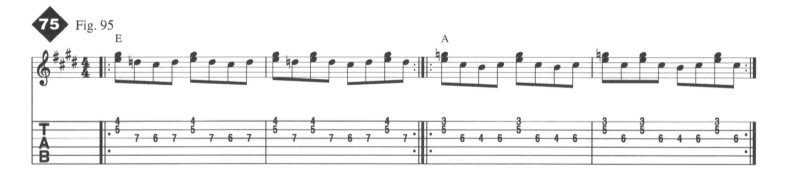

If you like the sound of cascading open-string runs, check out these next three repetitive licks over the I, IV, and V chords in the key of E:

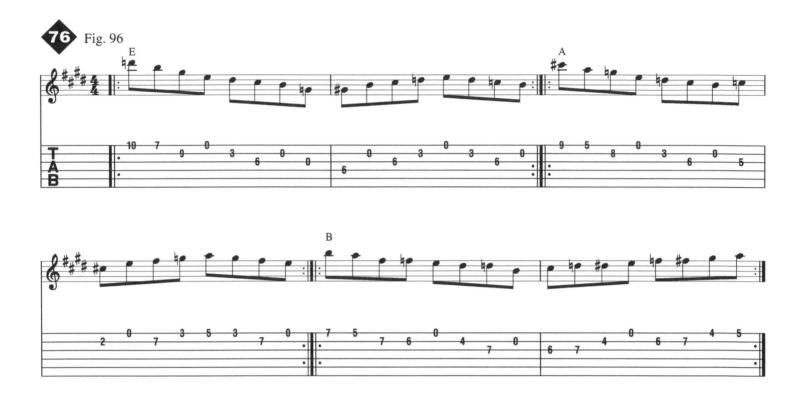

These licks outline the I, IV, and V chords in the key of D:

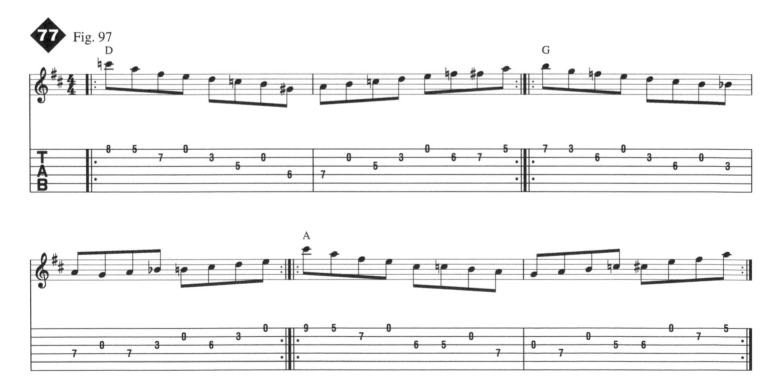

Chapter Six

CHROMATIC LICKS

The licks in this chapter contain chromatic *passing tones* (notes between the conventional scale tones). Try all of these licks in keys other than those of the examples.

The first example is a descending lick that begins on the fifth in the key of E:

The next example is an ascending lick that begins on the third in the key of D:

Here is an example in the key of E that begins with a chromatic run:

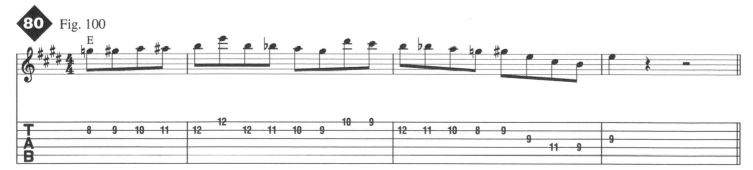

This lick, also in E, begins with an ascending chromatic run off the fifth and quickly descends to the third:

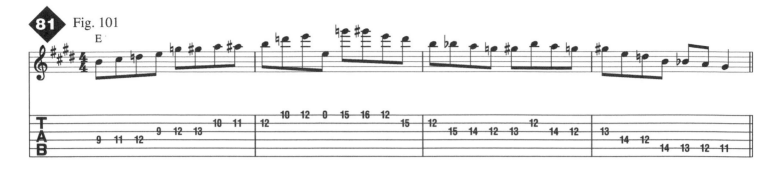

Try this ascending lick beginning on the root. This lick is less chromatic, yet still very effective.

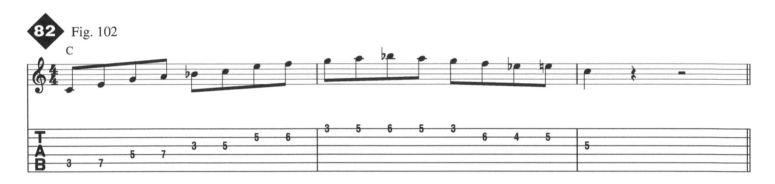

The next example begins with a chromatic line and jumps from the third to the first string, then descends with chromatic passing tones.

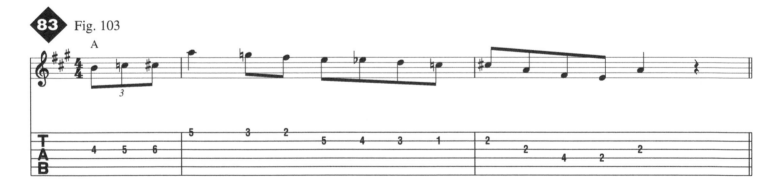

Here is a lick that weaves itself up and down chromatically, beginning on the fifth in the key of G.

This next lick is similar to the last one in that it begins on the fifth and descends chromatically, this time in A:

The next example ascends chromatically from the third, then winds its way back down to the root in the key of D:

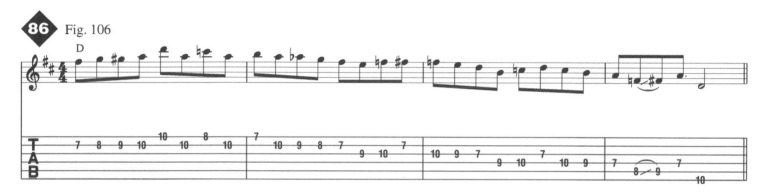

Here is a lick in E that begins on a passing tone (the flat third) and ascends with very few chromatic passing tones:

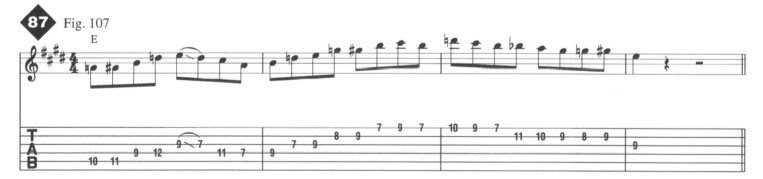

This next example is highly chromatic and highly challenging. It begins on the fifth and descends in the key of A.

Check out the way this next lick weaves its way down from the third on the first string to the root on the sixth string (in the key of A).

These next two licks incorporate some wider intervals. The first one begins on the root and ascends in the key of A.

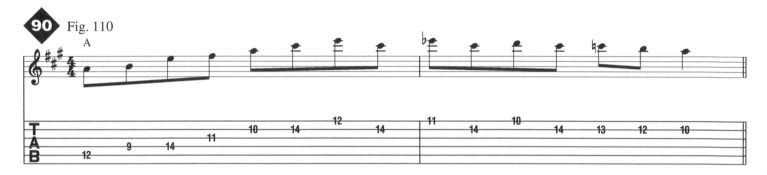

The second lick begins on the root and descends, also in A.

Here is a descending idea in the key of G, beginning on the fifth:

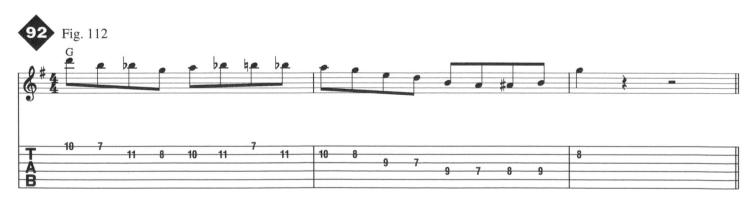

These next three examples sound great over swing-type tunes. They all incorporate wide intervallic leaps. The first lick, in the key of G, is rhythmically made up of triplets.

93 Fig. 113

The second lick is built off the third in the key of D.

94 Fig. 114

The third lick, also in D, is likewise built off the third, but is very different.

95 Fig. 115

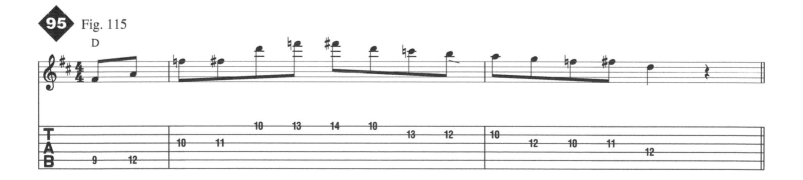

The next four licks cover a lot of ground very quickly. The first is in the key of E, and begins on the seventh:

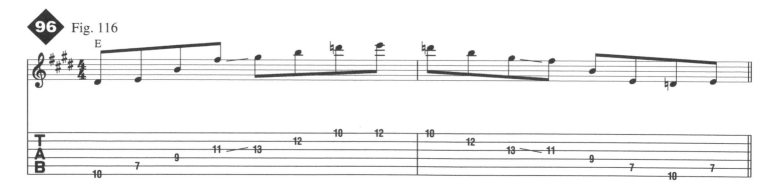

The second lick, also in E, begins on the third:

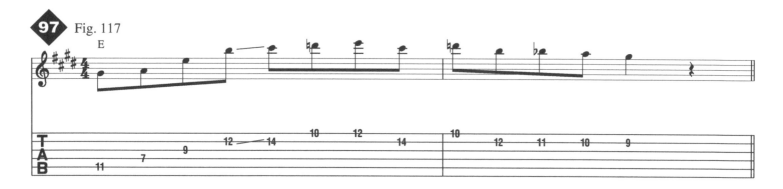

The third lick, again, is in the key of E, this time beginning on the fifth:

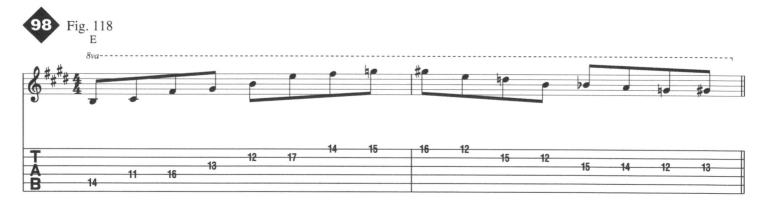

The fourth lick is in the key of A, and begins on the third:

Guitar Notation Legend

Guitar Music can be notated three different ways: on a *musical staff*, in *tablature*, and in *rhythm slashes*.

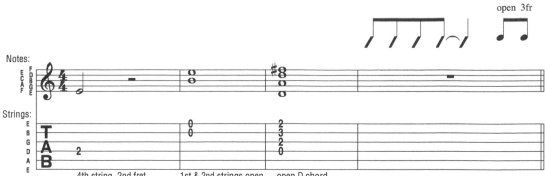

RHYTHM SLASHES are written above the staff. Strum chords in the rhythm indicated. Use the chord diagrams found at the top of the first page of the transcription for the appropriate chord voicings. Round noteheads indicate single notes.

THE MUSICAL STAFF shows pitches and rhythms and is divided by bar lines into measures. Pitches are named after the first seven letters of the alphabet.

TABLATURE graphically represents the guitar fingerboard. Each horizontal line represents a string, and each number represents a fret.

4th string, 2nd fret   1st & 2nd strings open, played together   open D chord

---

HALF-STEP BEND: Strike the note and bend up 1/2 step.

WHOLE-STEP BEND: Strike the note and bend up one step.

GRACE NOTE BEND: Strike the note and bend up as indicated. The first note does not take up any time.

SLIGHT (MICROTONE) BEND: Strike the note and bend up 1/4 step.

BEND AND RELEASE: Strike the note and bend up as indicated, then release back to the original note. Only the first note is struck.

PRE-BEND: Bend the note as indicated, then strike it.

VIBRATO: The string is vibrated by rapidly bending and releasing the note with the fretting hand.

WIDE VIBRATO: The pitch is varied to a greater degree by vibrating with the fretting hand.

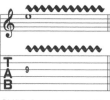

HAMMER-ON: Strike the first (lower) note with one finger, then sound the higher note (on the same string) with another finger by fretting it without picking.

PULL-OFF: Place both fingers on the notes to be sounded. Strike the first note and without picking, pull the finger off to sound the second (lower) note.

LEGATO SLIDE: Strike the first note and then slide the same fret-hand finger up or down to the second note. The second note is not struck.

SHIFT SLIDE: Same as legato slide, except the second note is struck.

TRILL: Very rapidly alternate between the notes indicated by continuously hammering on and pulling off.

TAPPING: Hammer ("tap") the fret indicated with the pick-hand index or middle finger and pull off to the note fretted by the fret hand.

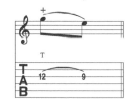

NATURAL HARMONIC: Strike the note while the fret-hand lightly touches the string directly over the fret indicated.

PINCH HARMONIC: The note is fretted normally and a harmonic is produced by adding the edge of the thumb or the tip of the index finger of the pick hand to the normal pick attack.

PICK SCRAPE: The edge of the pick is rubbed down (or up) the string, producing a scratchy sound.

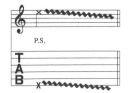

MUFFLED STRINGS: A percussive sound is produced by laying the fret hand across the string(s) without depressing, and striking them with the pick hand.

PALM MUTING: The note is partially muted by the pick hand lightly touching the string(s) just before the bridge.

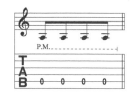

RAKE: Drag the pick across the strings indicated with a single motion.

TREMOLO PICKING: The note is picked as rapidly and continuously as possible.

VIBRATO BAR DIVE AND RETURN: The pitch of the note or chord is dropped a specified number of steps (in rhythm) then returned to the original pitch.

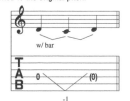

VIBRATO BAR SCOOP: Depress the bar just before striking the note, then quickly release the bar.

VIBRATO BAR DIP: Strike the note and then immediately drop a specified number of steps, then release back to the original pitch.

Guitar Instruction
Country Style!
from Hal Leonard

CHICKEN PICKIN' • by Eric Halbig

This book provides a "bird's-eye-view" of the techniques and licks common to playing hot, country lead guitar! Covers over 100 hot country guitar licks: open-string licks, double-stop licks, scales, string bending, repetitive sequences, and chromatic licks. The online audio includes 99 demonstration tracks with each lick performed at two tempos.

00695599 Book/Online Audio...$17.99

DANIEL DONATO –
THE NEW MASTER OF THE TELECASTER

PATHWAYS TO DYNAMIC SOLOS

This exclusive instructional book and DVD set includes guitar lessons taught by young Nashville phenom Daniel Donato. The "New Master of the Telecaster" shows you his unique "pathways" concept, opening your mind and fingers to uninhibited fretboard freedom, increased music theory comprehension, and more dynamic solos! The DVD features Daniel Donato himself providing full-band performances and a full hour of guitar lessons, The book includes guitar tab for all the DVD lessons and performances. Topics covered include: using chromatic notes • application of bends • double stops • analyzing different styles • and more. DVD running time: 1 hr., 4 min.

00121923 Book/DVD Pack $19.99

FRETBOARD ROADMAPS – COUNTRY GUITAR

The Essential Patterns That All the Pros Know and Use • by Fred Sokolow

This book/CD pack will teach you how to play lead and rhythm in the country style anywhere on the fretboard in any key. You'll play basic country progressions, boogie licks, steel licks, and other melodies and licks. You'll also learn a variety of lead guitar styles using moveable scale patterns, sliding scale patterns, chord-based licks, double-note licks, and more. The book features easy-to-follow diagrams and instructions for beginning, inter-mediate, and advanced players.

00695353 Book/CD Pack..$16.99

HOW TO PLAY COUNTRY LEAD GUITAR

by Jeff Adams

Here is a comprehensive stylistic breakdown of country guitar techniques from the past 50 years. Drawing inspiration from the timelessly innovative licks of Merle Travis, Chet Atkins, Albert Lee, Vince Gill, Brent Mason and Brad Paisley, the near 90 musical examples within these pages will hone your left and right hands with technical string-bending and rolling licks while sharpening your knowledge of the thought process behind creating your own licks, and why and when to play them.

00131103 Book/Online Audio..$19.99

COUNTRY LICKS FOR GUITAR

by Steve Trovato and Jerome Arnold

This unique package examines the lead guitar licks of the masters of country guitar, such as Chet Atkins, Jimmy Bryant, James Burton, Albert Lee, Scotty Moore, and many others! The online audio includes demonstrations of each lick at normal and slow speeds. The instruction covers single-string licks, pedal-steel licks, open-string licks, chord licks, rockabilly licks, funky country licks, tips on finger-ings, phrasing, technique, theory, and application.

00695577 Book/Online Audo $19.99

COUNTRY SOLOS
FOR GUITAR

by Steve Trovato

This unique book/audio pack lets guitarists examine the solo styles of axe masters such as Chet Atkins, James Burton, Ray Flacke, Albert Lee, Scotty Moore, Roy Nichols, Jerry Reed and others. It covers techniques including hot banjo rolls, funky double stops, pedal-steel licks, open-string licks and more, in standard notation and tab with phrase-by-phrase performance notes. The online audio includes full demonstrations and rhythm-only tracks.

00695448 Book/Online Audio............................$19.99

RED-HOT COUNTRY GUITAR

by Michael Hawley

The complete guide to playing lead guitar in the styles of Pete Anderson, Danny Gatton, Albert Lee, Brent Mason, and more. Includes loads of red-hot licks, techniques, solos, theory and more.

00695831 Book/Online Audio..$19.99

25 GREAT COUNTRY GUITAR SOLOS

by Dave Rubin

Provides solo transcriptions in notes & tab, lessons on how to play them, guitarist bios, equipment notes, photos, history, and much more. The CD contains full-band demos of every solo in the book. Songs include: Country Boy • Foggy Mountain Special • Folsom Prison Blues • Hellecaster Theme • Hello Mary Lou • I've Got a Tiger by the Tail • The Only Daddy That Will Walk the Line • Please, Please Baby • Sugarfoot Rag • and more.

00699926 Book/CD Pack...$19.99